The Incredible Whale

and Other Poems

Written by Helen Dineen

Illustrated by Svabhu Kohli and Juanita Londono

Collins

The Incredible Whale

What an incredible whale!
It sings us a magical song.

A giant of mythical tales,
The deep sea is where it belongs.

While waves whisk and foam as we go,
And winds whip our sailboat for miles,

4

Whenever a whale swims below,
It makes our adventure worthwhile.

Please, Sir!

Please, Sir, I feel very strange!
I think I need a nurse.

I had a little lie-down,
But it's only getting worse.

I've grown a set of whiskers ...

... and my words are squeaky too ...

... I've got a lovely tail,
You won't believe me – but it's true!

Yes, Sir, I feel very strange,
You've got to help me, please.

I've turned into a mouse!

I must have eaten too much cheese!

Uncle Mitch and the Terrible Itch

My Uncle Mitch had a terrible itch,
An itch on the tip of his nose.

But scratching that itch did him no good at all ...

... for it chuckled and ambushed his toes!

"I'll catch you, I'll snatch you!" he said to that itch (that itch that had ambushed his toes).

But when he bent over to scoop up that itch …

... it quickly hopped back to his nose!

My Fantastic "Ph" Poem

There are plenty of words that have "ph" in,
Like "photo" and "trophy" and "phew" ...

... and "alphabet", "dolphin" and "earphones",

and "geography", "graph" and "typhoon".

But you'll never find "ph" sounding better, than in —

Philippa Phyllis MacPhee

You'll find them right there, on my label,
Those words that describe only ME!

19

The Pebble

I found a polished pebble
that had settled in the sand.
Cool and smooth as marble,
I weighed it in my hand.
With tiny streaks of purple,
And flecks of snowy white,

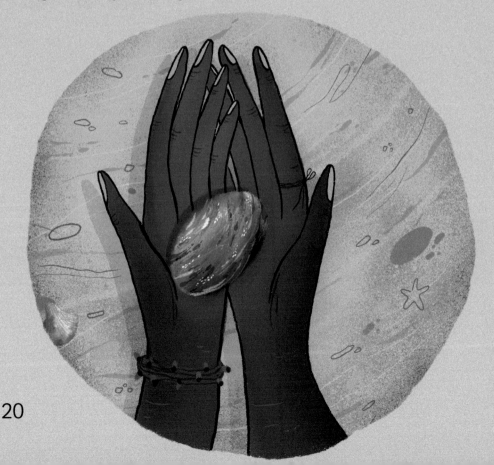

It sparkled as it whirled and spun ...

... then disappeared from sight.

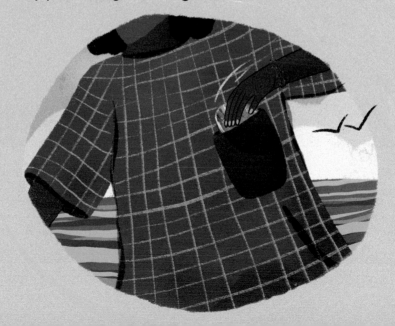

Pick a poem

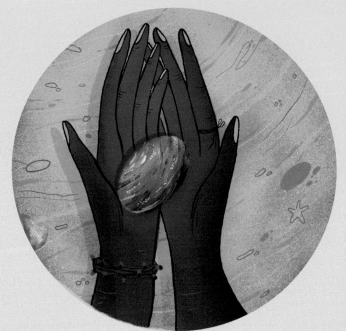

After reading

Letters and Sounds: Phase 5

Word count: 298

Focus phonemes: /ai/ a, eigh /ee/ e, y /oo/ u /igh/ ie, y /ch/ tch, t /j/ g, ge /l/ le /f/ ph /w/ wh /v/ ve /s/ se /z/ se

Common exception words: of, to, the, into, are, said, our

Curriculum links: Science: Animals, including humans; Art and design

National Curriculum learning objectives: Reading/word reading: apply phonic knowledge and skills as the route to decode words, read accurately by blending in unfamiliar words containing GPCs that have been taught, read other words of more than one syllable that contain taught GPCs, read words with contractions, and understand that the apostrophe represents the omitted letters; Reading/comprehension: develop pleasure in reading, motivation to read, vocabulary and understanding by: learning to appreciate rhymes and poems, and to recite some by heart, discussing word meanings, linking new meanings to those already known

Developing fluency

- Your child may enjoy hearing you read the book.
- Take turns to read a poem. Check that your child pauses for the dash on page 9 and ellipses (…) to add drama.

Phonic practice

- Focus on same spellings with different sounds. Ask your child to read these words. Which "se" spellings have the /z/ sound?

  mouse   nurse   worse   please   cheese

- Ask your child to read these words and identify the sound made by the letter "y".

  snowy   mythical   very   my   Phyllis   squeaky

Extending vocabulary

- Show your child these words with apostrophes. Can they tell you each phrase in full?

  I've (*I have*)   won't (*will not*)   I'll (*I will*)   you'll (*you will*)

- Can your child shorten these phrases using an apostrophe?

  I would (*I'd*)   she would (*she'd*)   there will (*there'll*)   that would (*that'd*)